# Survivors

Brooke S. Pisarsky

Illustrations by Derrick Williams

1   2   3   4   5   6   7   8   9   10

ISBN 0-8250-4971-1

Copyright © 2004

Walch Publishing

P. O. Box 658 • Portland, Maine 04104-0658

walch.com

Printed in the United States of America

# Survivors

# Table of Contents

## Introduction

What would you do to survive? There are many different types of survivors. Some people just need to hang on until help comes. Others are forced to do shocking things to save their lives.

Many times, people battle Mother Nature or disease. Those who fight the elements—such as floods, storms, or fires—need to act quickly to survive.

Sometimes, surviving means keeping still and quiet. That way an enemy cannot find you. And sometimes you fight not just for your own life. Others may be depending on you for their survival. In these cases, survivors may also become heroes.

In these six stories, you will meet all sorts of true survivors. Imagine what you would do in their shoes. How would you react? Could *you* survive?

Susanna Dickinson held her breath in the darkness. She hugged her 15-month old baby, Angelina, close. The child's whimpers grew quieter. The blast of rifles echoed through the tiny room. She cupped her hands over her daughter's ears and bent her head close. The shooting had been raging for more than an hour. "It'll be all right," she whispered. She was not sure she believed herself. It was March 6, 1836. Beyond the small room, the Battle of the Alamo was in full swing.

There were others in the dark room with her. Many were slaves of those who were fighting. Others were wives or sisters. Some were African-American, and some were Mexican. All were scared for their lives. Susanna was the wife of Almeron Dickinson. He was one of the brave men fighting to hold the Alamo. She wondered if she would ever see him again. The last time they had spoken had been brief. He had cried to her, "Great God, Sue, the Mexicans are inside our walls! All is lost! If they spare you, save my child." She aimed to do her best.

At times, the gunfire was deafening. Susanna and the others strained to hear voices they knew. They waited for the cheer that would mean that they had won. It would mean that Mexican President Santa Anna had backed down. With each hour, their hopes of hearing that cheer grew fainter. *Please,* she thought, *please let us get out of here alive. Please let my baby be safe.*

There was a break in the fighting. A brief silence followed. A Mexican voice was raised. "Where is the white woman?" a man asked. The door opened. A tall Mexican man stood in the doorway. Susanna squinted in the sudden light. Angelina hid her face in her mother's dress. General Juan Almonte, Santa Anna's right-hand man, pointed at her. In accented English he asked, "Are you Mrs. Dickinson?" "Yes," Susanna answered. "If you wish to save your life, follow me," he barked.

Susanna looked at the dark faces around her. Why her? Where was her husband? She rose to her feet. She held Angelina on her hip. She walked to the door and peered out.

Her eyes saw destruction. Susanna followed
General Almonte. Dead men lay where they
had fallen. Susanna watched in horror as
four Mexicans tossed one Alamo defender
in the air and shot him. Bullets rushed by
her. She quickened her step. She pushed her
daughter's head to her chest. There was so
much blood, so much death. She could hear
the groans of wounded men who would
never be healed. The air smelled like
gunpowder. Susanna did not know where
she was being taken. She dared not ask.
Perhaps she was to be a prisoner.

The battle was ending. The defenders
had been outnumbered. There had only been
182 of them. The Mexicans had come by the

thousands. Susanna knew, in her heart, that her husband must be dead.

Susanna hurried to catch up to the general. All of a sudden, there was a sting and then burning pain in her thigh. She had been shot! She stumbled, gripping Angelina. Susanna cried out, limping after Almonte. Tears of pain streamed down her cheeks. She tightened her grip on her child. At least her baby had not been harmed.

At last, after much painful walking, Susanna stood before Mexican President Santa Anna. The leader lifted Angelina to his lap. He pinched her chubby cheeks. Susanna's blood ran cold. This monster was holding her child! Santa Anna stroked the girl's hair and glanced at her mother. A sly grin spread over his face. The dictator offered Susanna a deal. He would take both Susanna and the baby to Mexico. There he would provide the best for Angelina. Susanna's mind spun. How dare he sit there with the fresh blood of Texas soldiers on his hands! She glared at him and refused.

Though she said no, Santa Anna spared her life. He made Susanna his messenger.

She was to carry a letter to Texan General Houston in Gonzales. The letter would declare Mexico's victory at the Alamo. It would also act as a warning to other Texans who thought of resisting Mexico's rule.

Susanna and the other female survivors were freed. They were each given a blanket and two dollars in silver. Susanna was given the letter. She and Angelina were put into the care of General Almonte's slave, Ben. They were joined by a former slave named Joe. Together, the three adults and one child started a long, dusty trip in an ox-cart. They stopped only for food and water. The letter from Santa Anna burned in Susanna's hand. It was tragic news to deliver. She hated helping the man who had killed so many. She looked at her sleeping child. That was her reason. Her baby was alive and safe. That was what mattered now.

It was dark by the time the small group reached Houston's camp. Susanna told her sad tale and handed Santa Anna's letter to Houston. Around her, women pressed her for details. Did she have a last word from this one's husband? Had she seen that one's brother? Susanna shared what she could, but her knowledge was scant. She closed her eyes. The scenes from the Alamo played in her head. These images would haunt her for the rest of her life. But she had escaped with her life and her child. Susanna remembered her husband's last words to her. *The Alamo has fallen,* she thought. *But I have kept my husband's last wish. Our child is safe.*

# Race Against Fire

The fateful day dawned just like all the
rest that summer. There had been
almost no rain for a month. Farms and

forests were thirsty for water. Scrap wood, left behind by loggers, baked in the late summer sun. Ashes from passing trains often set this tinder on fire.

That summer there had been lots of fires. Two were still burning just five miles from town. People were used to the haze of smoke in the air and the taste of ash in their mouths. But no one was prepared for the inferno when it came. It was September 1, 1894. That day, Hinckley, Minnesota, changed forever.

The two small fires outside Hinckley met and became one huge blaze. It roared toward the town. It ate all things in its path. The heat increased, turning the fire even more fierce. By mid-afternoon, the firestorm burst into town. There was no time to react. The people of Hinckley had to make quick decisions—or burn. Many choked on the smoke. Others grabbed their families and headed for swamps or gravel pits. There they hoped they would be safe below the water. Others tried to outrun the blaze. They ran north along the train tracks.

Engine 69 was a Limited Number 4 passenger train. It had begun its route south from Duluth earlier that day. Throughout the run, the crew had seen many small fires. Like the people of

Hinckley, the trainmen were used to such sights. But the passengers on Engine 69 were worried. The hot blasts of air and growing darkness alarmed them.

At the throttle sat Engineer James Root. He, too, had noticed the strange darkness. He, too, worried about what it might mean. As the train topped Big Hinckley Hill, he saw people running toward the train. "There must be something wrong in Hinckley," he said. He saw no fire, but he heard shouting. People yelled, "For God's sake, save us!" Root swiftly brought the train to a halt. He, his crew, and the other passengers helped over 150 people to board. There were now 300 people on the overloaded train.

As the last of the rescued townspeople boarded, fire exploded into the clearing. Root's face ran with sweat. His fireman, Jack McGowan, saw a tower of flame coming toward the train. "We can't stay here," he urged. "We have to get somewhere safe." Root scanned the burning land. He saw no more people. The tracks began to glow from the intense heat. The path in front of the train was now blocked by a wall of fire. Root's pulse raced and his heart pounded. *Going forward would be death,* he thought. *There's no choice but to go back the way we came.* Root threw the train into reverse. Skunk Lake, a marshy swamp, lay five miles to the north. They might find safety there.

Flames licked the train. The wooden sleepers—supports—on the tracks were burning. The train cars rocked, coming close to derailing. Then there was an explosion. A wave of fire struck the west side of the train! Windows shattered, spraying glass. A shard of glass struck Root in the neck. Blood gushed from the wound. Root was so focused on his work that he felt nothing. He could hardly see through the smoke. The fire was now on all sides of the train. Still Root held on, determined to reach Skunk Lake. The train traveled on, backward, away from the charred waste of Hinckley.

Damp towels were passed out to the passengers. They used them to put out the small fires that ignited on people's clothes. The towels also helped with breathing. Flames squeezed through every crack. The train seats smoked. Lamps burst. Some people fainted. Many prayed. Most were unsure if they would survive.

Root wobbled at the throttle. The heat and smoke were taking their toll. Twice he passed out from the fumes in the air. His clothes caught fire, but he took no notice. Luckily, McGowan saw the flames. He doused the engineer with water. Root's body ached from his grip on the throttle. His breathing was shallow. *I don't know if I can go much further,* he thought. He gathered his will to keep from passing out again.

With most of its cars on fire, Engine 69 finally reached Skunk Lake. Root pulled the train to a stop. He ordered his crew to help the people to water. Frenzied passengers rushed toward the swamp. Barbed wire stood in their way, but men pulled it apart with their bare hands. Into the murky waters they plunged.

Faint from loss of blood and from inhaling smoke, Root was too weak to follow. He slumped over the throttle, unconscious. McGowan and another crewman pried Root from his spot. The skin from Root's palms stayed on the lever. His eyebrows had burned and most of his hair was gone. But he was still alive.

McGowan and his helper dragged Root to the water just in time. Three waves of fire rushed over the crowd. Screams filled the air as people huddled under pieces of dampened cloth. They sank into the water to avoid the flames. Suddenly, the wind shifted. The fire died down. Ashes fell to the ground, sizzling. Relief swept over the group crouched in the foul water. They had been saved!

But not all were so lucky. The Great Hinckley Fire destroyed more than six towns. The smoke and flames claimed the lives of more than 400 people. Thanks to

James Root's quick thinking and his courageous crew, the passengers of Engine 69 escaped with their lives.

**S**he had been a good ship. But there was no saving her. The date was November 21, 1915. The 28-man crew of the

*Endurance* watched as she was crushed between ice floes—large chunks of floating ice. Down into the cold Antarctic waters she sank.

The *Endurance* had entered an ice pack about four months after leaving England. A month later, she was completely locked in. The ship creaked and jumped for weeks as the ice squeezed her. On October 27, the crew abandoned ship. They made camp on the ice and waited for the ship to sink. Now she was gone.

The crew, led by Sir Ernest Shackleton, was trapped on an ice pack in the Antarctic. Before the ship sank, the men had saved three tons of food stores, their 69 sled dogs, three lifeboats, and Frank Hurley's photography gear. They had survived 281 days on the ice-locked *Endurance*. The ship had drifted 1,186 miles. Most of those miles were north of the team's destination: Antarctica. The hardy crew, under Shackleton's command, had set out to be the first team to cross the continent on foot. With the loss of their ship, the chances of success were slim.

For four months, the men camped on ice floes. The dogs hauled the sleds filled with supplies. The men dragged the boats. With no open water, the lifeboats were a heavy burden. It was a risky trek. At times, the ice would break into pieces. Once this took place at night. Two men dropped through a crack that had opened under them as they slept. Luckily, they were rescued with no injuries. Food supplies dwindled. Although it was summer, it was cold. The men's clothes were worn. Their linen tents were nearly see-through.

March arrived. The men hunted for food. The easiest animal to catch was the penguin. If the men were lucky, they killed a seal. Food became so scarce that Shackleton gave a difficult order. The crew's beloved dogs were to be shot and eaten. Many men were sickened by the idea, but food was food—and they were starving.

Shackleton knew that he must get his men to land. But they were at the mercy of the ice. As long as they were trapped in the ice, they could not use their boats. Each day the ice drifted farther north. Finally, at the start of April 1916, they reached open water. The men piled into the lifeboats. They set course for Elephant Island, a speck of land 100 miles north. Steering around the ice floes was tricky. The floes could quickly come together, crushing anything between them. After much paddling and many hard nights

 spent in the violent water, the three boats made land. Shackleton wrote in his diary, "Thus, after a year's incessant battle with the ice, we had returned . . . to almost the same latitude we had left with such high hopes and aspirations twelve months previously!" They had faced so much danger and hardship. And they wound up back where they started.

The men were glad to be on solid ground. But Elephant Island offered no shelter or food. And the crew had no way of contacting the outside world. They had no radio. They were stranded where no ships might pass. Shackleton knew that rescue would not come to them. He formed a small group to find help. Shackleton chose five of his hardiest men to join him on the largest of the lifeboats, the *James Caird*. They prepared to sail for the nearest occupied land, South Georgia Island, where there was a whaling station. To get there, the group would need to cross 800 miles of the world's most violent water at the height of winter.

Shackleton chose Frank Wild, his second in command, to lead the group that stayed on Elephant Island. Shackleton knew that Wild could keep the men focused on survival. Wild had the men set up camp. With no trees, the men used rocks to form walls. On top of these walls they placed their two lifeboats, upside down. Inside, they lined the walls with sails for insulation. The shelters were not comfortable. But they would keep the men alive.

Meanwhile, the crew of the *James Caird* fought the rough waters of the Weddell Sea. Frank Worsley, the former captain of the *Endurance,* steered the lifeboat. He used a tool called a sextant to keep on course. But the sextant could only be used when the sun was out. They saw the sun only four times during the trip. Worsley somehow steered them in the right direction.

The men's worn clothes were frozen through. Their legs were covered in sores where their wet pants rubbed wet skin. Water constantly splashed into the open boat and froze. This ice created dangerous weight. The men dumped what they could to lighten the load. They chipped at the ice. On their seventh day at sea, the crew of the *James Caird* had some good luck. The sun came out and the temperature rose. The men hung their sleeping bags from the mast. They laid out their socks and what clothing they could spare. The ice began to melt.

On the eleventh day, a huge wave slammed the small boat. It was picked up, tossed, and flooded with water. The men bailed for their lives. The sea seemed to be against them.

After fourteen harrowing days at sea, they saw South Georgia Island. It would take the crew three more days to find a spot for landing. Because of the boat's battered state and two ill men, the crew was forced to land on the western coast. On May 10, 1916, the *James Caird* pulled ashore. Alas, once on ground, they were still 20 miles from the Stromness Whaling Station. The men would have to trek through the middle of the mountainous island. This had never been done because of the extreme terrain and weather.

Ten days after landing, Shackleton, Worsley, and Tom Crean set out for the station. The two ill men were too weak to go on. Shackleton left them with a third man, Timothy McCarthy.

The three men walked for 36 hours without stopping. Bone-weary and freezing, they pushed on. Several times they went one way only to realize that they had gone off track. They slid down slopes and walked through frigid water. At last, they reached the whaling station. The three men were unrecognizable. Once they explained who they were, the whalers welcomed them. They washed, ate, and slept. But their stay was brief.

Worsley went to get the three men left on the western coast. Shackleton wanted to get back to those on Elephant Island. But fate worked against him once more. For four months, Shackleton, Worsley, and Crean tried to get to Elephant Island on borrowed boats. Each time, the ice forced them back. It wasn't until their fourth try, aboard the Chilean steamer *Yelcho,* that they succeeded. But Shackleton worried that there would be no one left to rescue. The men left behind had been on their own for 105 days.

# The Shackleton Expedition

On the island, the steamer was spotted. The men lit a fire. They crowded along the icy beach. From the boat, Shackleton counted men through binoculars. "They are all there!" he cried. As the *Yelcho* drew near, Shackleton called out to Wild, "Are you all well?" Wild called back, "All safe, all well!" Within an hour, the crew was reunited. On August 30, 1916, the crew of the lost *Endurance* began their journey home. They had been away for more than two years.

**D**r. Jerri Nielsen was recently divorced and no longer saw her children. She needed something different in her life. An expert emergency room doctor, she wanted to use her skills in a new way. In a medical journal, she found that opportunity. It was an ad seeking doctors to live at a science base for a year—in Antarctica. She signed on as the sole doctor for the Amundsen-Scott South Pole Station. Before leaving, she had a full physical. The organization she would work for, the National Science Foundation (NSF), wanted to make sure that she was in top shape. Jerri passed with flying colors. By November 1998, Dr. Nielsen was settling into her new home at the bottom of the world.

Then life threw her a curveball. In

early March 1999, Jerri found a hard, lumpy mass in one of her breasts. At first, she was not concerned. It might be harmless. But when the mass began to grow, Jerri knew something was wrong. Very wrong. This lump could be cancer.

To add to Jerri's worries, the Antarctic winter was beginning. The continent shut down. Most people left. Night lasted for six months. The temperatures dipped below $-100°$ F. Planes were not allowed to fly in the area. The freezing temperature turned jet fuel to jelly. The South Pole is the windiest, coldest, driest continent. Over 97 percent of it is covered in ice. Jerri was stuck at the base until her year was up. But in that time, the cancer could spread.

For three months, Jerri kept the lump a secret. Since no plane could come until the end of October, death was likely. Then, she decided that she owed the truth to her coworkers. After all, they had become like family. She told her boss first. He urged her to contact her doctor in the States. Her doctor said that Jerri would need to get a biopsy. A biopsy is a removal of tissue for study. As she was the only doctor, Jerri would have to do it herself.

She knew that she needed help. With a

heavy heart, she broke the news to her fellow "South Polies." Jerri asked the team's welder, a former Army medic, to help her with the biopsy. They trained on yams, fruit, and a chicken breast. For the procedure, Jerri was awake. She used only ice and a local painkiller to help her through. Once the biopsy was done, another Polie rigged up an old microscope to the computer. This let Jerri e-mail her biopsy slides to her doctor. The answer came back. Jerri did have breast cancer. And there was a 50 percent chance that it would kill her.

Jerri now had to tell her friends and family back home. The only way to do this was by e-mail. Jerri hated to break bad news in such a distant way. She sent off an e-mail with the subject "Serious Medical Problem at Pole." Her brother later said that he thought the e-mail would be about Jerri saving someone's life. He never dreamed it would be about the possible end of her own.

Jerri's doctor wanted her to start chemotherapy. Despite the harsh weather, the NSF sent a plane to fly over the research station. Cancer-fighting drugs were dropped in large crates. Finding all the boxes in the 24-hour night was a challenge. Once they were found, Jerri trained her team to help with the process.

Together they learned how to mix the drugs. Everything had to be exact. They all hoped that the chemo would stall the cancer.

The lump started shrinking. Jerri and the Polies began to hope. But then the medicine seemed to stop working. The lump grew bigger. The chemo made Jerri's hair fall out. She grew very ill. Even after the drugs were changed, Jerri's health worsened. She got ready to die. She found peace in the fact that this last year had been so new and exciting.

Her doctor was in favor of Jerri being rescued. Jerri wondered if it would be

worth
it. She
knew that
the prognosis—
her chances for
survival—was poor. She did not want to
risk the lives of her would-be rescuers.
But the station needed a healthy doctor.
The NSF wanted to get Jerri out and get a
new doctor in. An Air National Guard LC-
130 plane would try to reach her. The ski-
equipped LC-130 was the only type of
plane able to land on the frozen continent.
The rescue would take place at the
beginning of October. This was more than

two weeks before flying was thought to be safe.

Most of the Polies did not think the rescue was possible. Not only is the Antarctic climate brutal, all that white can confuse a pilot. There have been many cases of a pilot thinking he was headed in one direction, when he was aiming straight for a land mass. This mission would be dangerous.

Once the plane arrived on the north coast of Antarctica, it needed to wait until temperatures at the station rose to at least −58° F. At last, on October 16, 1999, the LC-130 made it to the South Pole. Jerri and her fellow Polies were ready. They had only minutes to get Jerri into the plane. To wait any longer would be to risk the LC-130 freezing. The plane kept its engines running as the switch was made. With her friends' help, Jerri scrambled into the plane as the new doctor got off. The entire rescue took just 22 minutes.

Jerri was rushed to Christchurch, New Zealand, and then to the United States. Her cancer was treated. She has since had many surgeries. She reports being cancer-free. In one interview, Dr. Nielsen was asked if she would ever go back to the South Pole. She said, "I would go back tomorrow if I could!" The cancer may have scarred her body, but her spirit remains strong and intact.

At 3:00 P.M. on Wednesday, July 24, 2002, two crews of nine men entered the Quecreek Mine in Pennsylvania. The

first crew headed straight down the main shaft. The second crew climbed onto the mine car. They headed into a side shaft. The coal seam they were working was about a mile and a half from the mine entrance. It was 245 feet below ground. This shaft was cutting toward the abandoned Saxman Mine. Still, the crew knew they were safe. Their maps showed that the Saxman Mine was hundreds of feet of solid earth away.

The crew knew each other well. They also knew coal mines. Many of them were the sons, grandsons, and brothers of miners. Robert Pugh, with 31 years as a miner, had the most experience. Harry

Mayhugh, with just over five years, had the least. Crew chief Randy Fogle, the son and grandson of miners, had been a miner for 22 years. Between them, the nine men had spent over 200 years in the mines.

The shafts they worked in were about 4 feet high and about 20 inches wide. The miners wore headlamps in the pitch-black maze of shafts. Just before 9:00 that night, Mark Popernack was near the end of the shaft. The machine chewed coal from the wall ahead. Suddenly, the machine vanished in a wall of water. The maps had been wrong! The old Saxman Mine was closer than they had thought. And it had filled with water. Now that water—

millions of gallons—spewed into the Quecreek Mine!

The men moved quickly. Dennis Hall was closest to the mine phone. He called the other crew. "The water's on the way," he yelled. "Get out!" That crew dropped everything and ran for the mine entrance. The tunnel flooded so quickly that many had to escape through neck-high water.

Back at the breach, Randy Fogle's crew battled for their lives. The shafts filled up quickly. The men were already bent over because of the low ceiling. The water was at their necks. Mayhugh, over six feet tall, was crouched almost in half.

The crew slogged through the flood toward the mine entrance. But the water became too high. They had to turn back. They went through the small networks of tunnels. Using cement blocks already in the mine, they tried to build a wall to seal off some of the passageways. The work was hard. Some men got sick. The air in the Saxman Mine was toxic. The men were breathing low-oxygen air known as "black damp."

After they had finished four walls, the water pushed in. The men moved to higher ground. They found a damp hill that the water didn't completely reach. The men gathered in the dark. They had

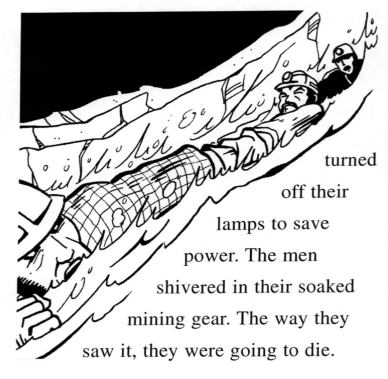

turned off their lamps to save power. The men shivered in their soaked mining gear. The way they saw it, they were going to die.

Topside, officials arrived on the scene less than an hour after the mine wall broke. At the mine entrance, heavy-duty machines pumped out the flooded mine.

# Flood Underground: The Quecreek Miners

They moved 12,000 gallons of water per minute. Rescuers figured out where the miners might have found safety. To do this, they used high-tech Global Positioning System (GPS) equipment. Crews began drilling a 6-inch-wide airhole down to the miners. Rescue crews had to move swiftly. This was a race against time. No one knew if the miners were even still alive. Often, those trapped in a mine die before rescue efforts even begin. Experts guessed that the mine air was near 55° F. Even if the miners were still alive, the cold could cause them to pass out.

Finally, the drill broke through! The

rescue crew heard tapping from down below. Someone was alive! The crew tapped a response. Workers pumped heated, compressed air down the shaft. The compressed air formed an air bubble. This kept the water at bay. It also brought oxygen to the men. Cheered, the rescue crew began the next phase. They prepared to drill a 2-foot-wide rescue shaft. For this, they would need a powerful drill. A "super drill" was rushed to the scene from West Virginia. It was set up and put to work at once. The crew predicted that it would take 18 hours to reach the trapped men.

The town gathered close. Prayer vigils

were held for the nine miners. Family members were comforted. Governor Mike Schweiker pumped up the rescue workers with his positive words. "Our working notion is we're on a rescue mission," he told the press. "We're going to bring our nine guys out."

Down below, the miners tried to keep up each other's spirits. But the cold and damp made it hard. At one low point, the men scribbled last words to loved ones on cardboard. They tucked these notes into a waterproof bucket that they nailed to a wall. Thomas Foy grabbed a mining cable. He looped it through all of their belts. He explained that they were going to live or die as a team.

Hunger gnawed at them. Hall's lunch pail was the only one to survive the flood. He split his corned-beef sandwich nine ways. He shared his only can of Pepsi. Foy found a couple of bottles of soda that he passed around. Sugar, they hoped, would keep them awake. To beat back the cold, they tried to cover themselves with canvas from the mines, but it did little to warm them.

Early Friday morning, there was a setback topside. The drill bit suddenly broke. The workers were only halfway down. A replacement bit would need to be flown in.

The miners worried about the abrupt silence. Had the rescuers given up? Most of the men fell into despair. Their boss waved their worries away. "Ah, they might have plugged up or broken a bit," he said. No one really believed him. Their hopes plunged.

By Friday night, drilling on the shaft started again. By dawn on Saturday, workers thought that they were within 60 feet of the trapped men. At this point, the drillers would have to go on with care. If they broke the air bubble, the water could flood the miners' small safe space. The drilling slowed, taking most of the day.

The men in the mine saw the water level falling. They listened with joy as the drilling once more began and came closer. At last the drill appeared! The men, both above and below ground, cheered. Soon a microphone was lowered to the miners.

As soon as the miners had the microphone, they spoke to the rescue crew. The workers up top learned that all nine men were alive and well. "What took you so long?" asked a raspy, laughing voice. It was 10:30 P.M. The Quecreek miners were about to be rescued.

Randy Fogle had been having chest

pains, so he was pulled up first. Ten minutes later, Mayhugh took his turn in the basket. Each rescue took between 10 and 15 minutes. Mark Popernack was the last miner out, at 2:44 A.M. People cheered and clapped as each miner, filthy with coal, was lifted out. Each man was bundled into a waiting ambulance or helicopter.

Though the Quecreek miners were underground for more than four days, none suffered life-threatening conditions. Most were released within a day or two of the rescue. Some have hung up their hard hats for good. Others have braved the dangerous world of mining once more.

They are no longer a mining team, but in their hearts these survivors will always be crewmates.

**A**ron Ralston dangled from his ropes 60 feet above the ground. The 27-year-old adventure seeker had set out to do just this. He had already scaled most of Colorado's top peaks, often alone and in winter. The night before, he had driven to Utah's Horseshoe Canyon trailhead. He camped in his truck. That morning, Saturday, April 26, 2003, he rode his mountain bike along the trails. The stark landscape was both beautiful and eerie. He reached the trailhead to Bluejohn Canyon and tied his bike to a tree. Then he set out to do some canyoneering—climbing sideways in narrow canyons.

Bluejohn Canyon was perfect for this. It's a slot canyon. From above, it is a dark slash in the rock. It is barely a yard wide. Below the rim, the rock walls drop almost

100 feet.

In the slot, Aron used his gear to scale the inner face of the canyon. Each move was careful and practiced. Then he came to a huge rock wedged between the canyon walls. He tested it. Once he was sure it was firm, he began to climb over it. But the rock shifted. Aron tried to pull back. His right arm did not make it in time. Down came the 800-pound boulder, pinning his right hand. A scream tore out of Aron's throat as he felt the bones crush. He hurled his body at the rock, trying to free himself.

As the pain shifted to a dull numbness,

Aron tried to think of his options. One of four things could happen. He could be rescued. He could chip away at the boulder enough to free his hand. He could rig up some sort of lifting device with his gear. Or he could cut off his arm. He knew that death was a possibility, but he did not want to think about it.

Aron looked at his food. He had two burritos, one liter of water, and some candy bar crumbs. *I've got to be careful about the food,* he thought. Aron knew that he would have to eat to keep up his strength. Being a seasoned hiker, he also knew that his food would not last long.

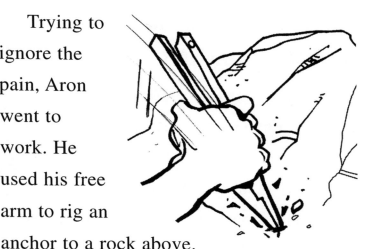

Trying to ignore the pain, Aron went to work. He used his free arm to rig an anchor to a rock above. He used his climbing gear to make a system of pulleys. Nothing worked. Next he grabbed his multitool. If he chipped at the point where the rock met the canyon wall, maybe he could move the rock and free his hand.

Evening fell. The temperature fell, too. In his shorts and T-shirt, Aron shivered.

But he kept working. He wore the blade down but barely chipped the rock.

For two days, Aron tried to free himself. On Tuesday, he sipped the last of his water and ate his remaining food. On Wednesday, he looked at his options again. His stomach rumbled. The dull pain in his crushed arm would flare up and then die down. No one had shown up to help him. The rock had not budged. Aside from dying, cutting off his arm was the last thing he could try. *I have to be realistic,* he thought. *If I want to get out of here, I have to cut off my arm.* Gritting his teeth, he got to work. He sawed at his arm with the blade of his multitool. But the blade was so dull, it didn't even break the skin. It would not cut through bone.

By Thursday, he was losing strength. *I have to do something before I get any weaker,* he thought. *Otherwise, even if I get out from under the rock, I'll never make it out of the canyon.* That's when an idea struck. He knew that his knife would not cut through bone. But what if he broke the bones first? Maybe he could cut through the skin and muscle.

Aron moved his body to get his arm in position. He bent it until it snapped— twice, once for each bone. He tied a tourniquet around his arm to stop the bleeding. Then he started to cut. *I can't think about the pain,* he thought. *I have to move on, just do what I have to do.*

An hour later, his arm was free. But Aron was still in the middle of nowhere, alone. He tied up the injured arm. Then he scrambled through the rest of the canyon. At the end of the canyon, he rigged a rope. He rappelled—one-armed—down a 60-foot rock face. Then he started hiking toward his truck.

Five miles later, he came upon a family of three Dutch tourists. They were Eric, Monique, and Andy Meijers. Aron cried out, "Help! I need help!" The three guessed he was the missing hiker that they had heard about. Monique and Andy ran ahead to get help quickly. Eric stayed behind to guide Aron.

Unknown to them, a search-and-rescue crew had been sent out. Monique and Andy Meijer saw the helicopter. They waved wildly. The deputies who landed the chopper were stunned. Aron was covered in blood. One deputy thought, *His red legs match the red rocks*. But he was walking on his own and speaking clearly. He was quickly flown to a hospital.

The deputies hiked into the canyon. They hoped they could get back Aron's hand. But when they saw the blood-splashed boulder, they knew it was hopeless. The rock weighed about 800 pounds. It took a team of 13 men with hoists and jacks to move the rock.

Despite the loss of his right arm, Aron has not changed his active life. Aron Ralston wrestled death and won.